ONE WOMAN-HORSE SHOW

Jess Murrain is a queer poet of British-Caribbean heritage working mainly in performance, live art and theatre. Her wider practice explores film-poetry and she is one of Southbank Centre's New Poets Collective 21/22. She is also co-founder of 'Theatre with Legs', an experimental company based in Bradford and London. *One Woman-Horse Show* is her debut poetry pamphlet.

One Woman-Horse Show

Published by Bad Betty Press in 2022
www.badbettypress.com

All rights reserved

Jess Murrain has asserted her right to be identified as the author of this work in accordance with Section 77 of the Copyright, Designs and Patents Act of 1988.

Cover illustration by Daniel Owusu

Printed and bound in the United Kingdom

A CIP record of this book is available from the British Library.

ISBN: 978-1-913268-29-9

ONE WOMAN-HORSE SHOW

*For Mum, Nan
and Katie*

After we have made the choice to be healed in love, faith that transformation will come gives us the peace of mind and heart that is necessary when the soul seeks revolution.

– bell hooks

Contents

Analogue 1980s	9
Girl	10
Rules against growing	12
Falling Short	14
Seaside	16
A Coke Float in a Dream	17
Jah	18
One in Four Cowboys Were Black	20
When she was	22
The Dressing Gown	23
Half	25
Of hidden frames	27
Women are living in drums	28
Into an impotent guilt	30
Evolution of a brother gone quiet	31
Out of Shot	32
Launderette & Ant	35
By the hour	36
No space for tiny dying	38
One Woman-Horse Show	39
Notes	44
Acknowledgements	45

Analogue 1980s

this was the nearest thing to church
your non-believing parents once agreed on
you could drive there in those days you were born
of this religion clubs with strange names
funkateers & boogie boys a communion wave
in its original form picket frequencies fires
through teenage letterboxes
straight from the microphone
of dual heritage laid onto mixed tape
you were born of a national health service
desire for widespread better
soon to be dismantled trainee nurses
who grooved to jazz-funk with your mother
called in sick for your mother
seven cantering Mondays
nurse Sal was known for taking
oranges & apples to the joint
save having to buy her skin a drink

Girl

the power of self-soothing. little legs. you holster your gun
to a rummaged belt and Warren next door wants to play out. fuck that.

pudding

is a 7p rocket lolly. onwards and daydream into the football shirt
of a filmic man. *Darling swig!* the rugged toil of lip, the honey tilt of glass.

regal sway

necking whiskey actually vinegar, performing my jeans *So this is how she
will kiss!* boy swig again, then

one time later move to pretend London, fall in love with someone
whose head got kicked in

in a toilet cubicle, aged 15. as you learn her name
people will hear your voice and place you in the wrong past.

there are never enough pockets to drip into the gaps of *explain*
what is disparate about your denim. love is recurring

with every outing of a hat. sufficiently waterproof
to be used as a bucket. this here nasty island.

the permanent state of childhood
in a game.
survival for a solo kid

lays quiet in the eyes.

hers
bluer than an easter egg.

Rules against growing
for Gen Z

desire & ball games
the worry of a trout
living inside your body.
take it to the floor
to dance. ageing is
collaborating
with all the thoughts
that stand you up. try
crying backwards, one
more pointless talent
pelvic girdles
catch on fire.
your groin remembers
you so break bread
with later lovers.
intimacy will never stabilise
& cartoons
tell close-up truth
like a man who's always hiding
in a crowd or
a cat will be a dog.
the consequence
of a long school tie.
salute the curls of appetite
all the way to the curving
future, burdened

by the bigger picture
THEKIDSARECOMING
THEKIDSARECOMING
THEKIDSARECOMING
demanding to learn
about empire. revolution
is returning
to the beginning.
the day the harm
broke free.

Falling Short

we walk the Yorkshire hills. we trial vowels
unravelling. yours are long-formed

over heather, something you call bracken
gnarls around us. palms relinquish their green.

these ferns die back to brown. i'm hunting
for my voice in a map. empty beer cans strewn

like omens. you can't swap grief for grief.
he's dead & the world is spinning on a different axis

yes mine are living—but they left me slowly over time
my body is a story chipped at daily.

know that these speeches fall short
of a longed for spirit. a small rain.

the circle is shaking. the smell of water.
I didn't leave you out of fear

let the leaves go, let them turn to mulch.
under our feet a stage. borrowed soil. plants.

*I left because you were hurting me. the bruises
playing out* live under birdie lights. we crawled.

it was easier swapping disco balls
or singing for the friends.

it was easier stealing chairs from churches.
they were orange & meant for children.

Seaside

I watch the music in my Dad's leg. the need to grip behind towels. itches in our stay away beds the militarization of picnic. sandwiches declare themselves desperate & as we sip on cheap cola a man on the fringes of himself is incarcerated for stealing a bicycle. we are born into a lie told over & over. a wave. so then let's raise our plastic to consumption. let's get the fuck out of our eardrums. I ran across a lifetime I wanted to tell you. bodies are left to drift. a wave. cameras don't capture Dad just the whites
of his holiday smile.
rinsing down my wrist

are deeply conservative variants
of lemon ice.
sugar
the biggest atrocity
on humankind's
tongue.

A Coke Float in a Dream

midnight floats like you bruised my living

all for the nothingness of starlings/mute movers

these iron filings will protect my bed

& children will find love in birds & insects.

return from your lates to stroke my head

one last Wednesday in the soft house

I'll bouncy-castle up, solitary sleep

in your pint-sticky arms.

speak me into being

like a favourite.

Jah

From the inside of cellos
& in the name of all Gods

                adult voices
loosen my sleep.

The dregs of 90s hip-hop interferes
with all I hope to do
in darkness

Label me greedy
                        but seldom seen

I journey down the ladder of my bed
the short walk to Mum & her friends

The volume in my gut & in this flat
as they re-hash my private homeland

                        Reverie is hanging onto dawn
& cassette tapes
heave a strange night

I'm aged nine & trying

The hunger of a pellet-gun
from the underside of my pillow

to the underside of my hand
I'm having visions   of leavin' here in a hearse

& in the thrill of this awake,
I find H

H, like me, is steadily returning
to Zion

*& whenever you let me hit it
sweet like honey* he is waiting   for deliverance

                                        H cheers me on,
                                        because I'm his champion
& in the name of all Gods   playmate
the man trusts me

to fire an empty beer can
off his head

One in Four Cowboys Were Black

ONE

It's confusing to text your love in plummet seconds. My peanut head. Search for a gun. A waving hand emoji in brown. She might not be able to reply goodbye in the time I negotiate. Falling people. A waste of a trigger. *You are my milky boy* is what she says to help me feel like a mountain. I've not held her. I've been crying with the moths.

IN FOUR

minutes, head to the bar. watch your friends get served before you. wait dog your wrists are on leashes your friends are all called Dom & all the Doms are proud & happy to buy you

a drink & a bit annoyed you're on edge   taking so long

                                                        to call him back

COWBOYS

wearing hair high an arrangement that revalorizes desire. swagger my afro
holding trinkets in this kink.

WERE BLACK

as if cowboys no longer exist.
a teacher points
to my brain
pretending
to laugh
is loading
my certificates
into barrels
I shoot them
into proof
like money
falls in films
my heaviness
a huge refuse sack
for all concerned
speaking bondage
kills a party
a brown paper
bag party
I dance
on the doorstep
outside I am bloody
good at dancing
dancing is what
we're good for

When she was

Shirley is without her glasses.
Fallen from her bed,
she's in the sapling position.
It's always the same
when you slink to the floor
the young girl inside thinking:
surely standing is easy?
It used to be breathing her way
up a Tina Turner song.
Existing only inside her jive.
& now her glasses, jet-streamed.
Her scanning hands lead to nowhere
but to the faith &
in a morning nearby

Shirley's grandchild
is recording joy, glasses on
& shape-groining
the world's biggest mimed wave.
her pelvis
is committed to her pleasure
as the carpet is to cigarettes.
O butter knives
la di dah. Place one
in nightwear la di dah.
A hot knees-up:
this sure is easy the scent
of playtime breeding
a myth.

The Dressing Gown

the animal body is invoked when fearful the animal body can't assume shadows
are safe to play with my grandmother gently unhangs the dressing gown

dismantling its folds from the threat of a face like any decent puppet it dies
when it hits the ground I address the dark anew pinching my pulse

and resting into the hope of birdsong a blank wall nothing hanging no priest
and I'm mopping up the wide of my eyes the wet on my pyjamas where bears

embrace thin on fading cotton keeping my panic company each bear
wrapping around her sibling clasping paws together is this survivors' guilt?

the questions cry themselves aloud like a train catching my body dragged under
I prise at figments of cloth I wonder is my imagination feral or is the gown

the man I will one day know to be my friend yes he will accompany me on drums
at a gig then home later to scour through his girlfriend's devices as she brews tea

camomile in their candlelit life he demands her passwords or in another London
he writes her into the night as she runs he dashes her into his novel

the dressing gown is wearing slogans of allyship under the dwindling
thud of a party the woman he raped in their student days

is still negotiating her relationship he begged her afterwards
to consider the route blood takes to the brain

organs reorganising themselves in the aftermath of a morning mine is lingering
past sleep leaving me to remember my grandmother listening by the door

she left ajar always believing surely this is love lighting up the sound
of the wood pigeon's call how do these birds pitch their song? blue note on a frost

Half

men ask my height
my body I splinter
who are you to be here

my queer hips
I make smaller
the space
inside my genitals

I turn
purposefully ghost
to be here
I also splinter
my mother

*

let's pick up the phone
to our respective mums
let's announce ourselves
alight on the blower

let's tell them
we are touching quietly
on top of kitchen units
hues of inherited retro

I will tell mine
she hasn't told her family
about me yet
since

white men
are easier
to introduce
into a life

and in a language
I crave to speak
yours might
agree

Of hidden frames

with mornings we enter water we rinse our bodies
shifting under a bathroom ceiling
the threat of crew cuts a makeshift shower
our night-clasp of confidence now jaded
so take me for a public breakfast please take me
for strong coffee forks are touching
I'm asking my hand to pass the ketchup
please is me asking you to frame me inside
I'm not demanding magenta
just hold my gaze in public
calm the mug the memory of alarm
in unmade beds alarms are nothing
but waking up knowing I have spilled myself
all over a book you said was life changing
in bed having swallowed our first second
cut to me wondering
is this the slowest I can chew

Women are living in drums

the skin of our lid
hides how damn well
I wear my trousers
it shelters my wrist
the bracelet
you loved outside.
you aren't here tonight
in our drum. you've left
to ponder the spirit
of gently poured wine.
it's almost the moment
& when the hour
strikes delicate
I shred at rawhide
step out of its animal
stitch it back together
& walk it cradled
like a baby lily I water
all the way
to the restaurant
holding my child
all the way to the table
where we will eat
with your father
& lie about the nature
of our relationship.
he notices our bracelet

asks after its origin
I drop my hand
mute it under knives.
I feel now
for leaves.

Into an impotent guilt

bubbles of speckled hen lady colonising & apologising simultaneously she yolks herself collars her dog infected pudding i smell cynical *University?* taped & bled answers *did you?* welded as a lung might ride the sea as a flag will act as bondage in my wake spotlighted i am nominated saviour by sweeting cluck bitch i am a bitch please get me there faster i wish to feel easy to lift or licked ice-cream Mother England sucks her liberal roses her Noddy cheeks *you have around you something I've never seen before* effervescence? say it to my *blackface. Leave.* me churning

Evolution of a brother gone quiet

driving into accidents
he is the boy who fell from a building site
down he died
to the sound of a saxophone
settling scores he couldn't play
as it turned out   the boy survived
is now living as jazz
my little brother

won't ask after his desires
held up against our father
bleeding lyricless   wringing his beard for seawater
my brother the baby
desperate   to scream   on a beach
he is withdrawing on a family
losing the will to hold my prolonged hand
I'm watching him watch

a Monday   we are returning
from our trip
the weight of   my quiet bundle
in arms   he is a teenager
beside the written word   feeding afternoons
inside his head   rests a library spitting bars
a sanctuary found
the man

Out of Shot

Two white men
are experimenting with a gun.
I'm riding the air
holstered, I'm on a horse.
My Smith & Wesson rubs
at my pelvis. It's the hottest
August on record & one eye
is with the woman I love.
I want to hold her losses, understand
her arms. We've been fucking
in secret for a year. A quiet
disposition means the director
enjoys my work ethic. She
doesn't know I drink real liquor
in this scene.

A white experiment
is a gun & two men.
He relished the invitation to fire
in the name of art, especially since
his friend had been wanting to draw
close. An ideal aim is 15ft away.
A nip. Blood creeping down
a limb, like an ant on a cone.
It didn't turn out that way.
The bullet spun through flesh.
A very American aesthetic
& this wound would become
his most famous.

Years later, I'm shot too
at close range
while waiting for my mother
in a car park.

Men, guns & whiteness
all started as experiments.
Married to rain, the concrete hums
of sugar-grit & oak. The hyacinths
frame the outside of Asda where I
will fall. The sky, my hot iron rod
bright & white & laying me off
like the bed sheets I'll never sleep on again.
A woman called Sarah is running
towards me.
She's the history I haven't.
She's forgotten her arthritis, her life
swollen with urine
is no daytime priority.
Sing me through the bars
Sarah. Sway me by the trunk
of our sorrow-body
like Dumbo.
Little one when you play
the bullet that landed in me
was searching for another.

White men separate
their bodies from the land.
They choose to own the same gun.
They smoke. Drink lemonade.

To die as disparate as I started
is to unpick silence. Inherited.
My many blood types.
I wish my mum was here.
She rode a pony called Honey
round the mountain
she drew her heart. Placed me
inside of it. Sarah sings
She'll be here soon baby
don' wurry. she'll be criss
& she'll be ridin'
she'll wearing pink pyjamas

Launderette & Ant

my machines pumping ylang ylang & for what *stay with your clothes* this one weary dolly / comes in on Tuesdays / her gold plimsolls & / she dreams as she spins of the smashed tomato / she was scolded for that steal in the supermarket aisle / her cousin laughed / as her mother hit-smacked her wrist raw / she will never eat a tomato again / one night her uncle was murdered at a soirée after she ate a BLT in fact / he was punched with a gold knuckle duster on the bridge of his nose / the tale lives a little flimsy like I never knew him myself / but apparently they all died not long after / & especially every time she ate some form of tomato / later the cousin slipped inside a glacier never to be seen again / I once met a man at a festival who got stuck inside an avocado to be fair / Ant ignores this / he crawls up & down my buckets like they're trash bags

Ant says, we don't have much time.

By the hour

he is calling his sister for help.
his tears perform stunts

over the dial tone
he's an infant. the sister answers, leans

into the sob. her questions a twitching
of fish. she directs him

to water, directs him to her place
on the other side of town

but she won't be there to open the door.
she's away and awake in the belly

of her lover's kitchen. her lover upstairs,
a field of strawberries, listening in.

the sister won't sleep by the hour.
the one necessary for denial. this is the brother

arriving finally, laying waste
to his loose change. the flatmate tucks him under

a duvet. notes their resemblance
as dawn is risking its shape

through the spare bedroom window
christ, your place reeks of dog flatmate

rolls this wet in her mouth;
it's time for morning oats.

No space for tiny dying

there is no moon tonight. this has its consequence. for you. it is something akin to glimpsing the flight path of monsters. sleeplessness is to grieve in small sections. dust by chisel. minutiae explosions happen to the right of your face. a communion of worry dolls accompany your skull. wince upon orbit. you're awake & twitching over gravity. how wordlessly you splinter in the dark. supposing you only have forty years left to lick parch-pink rock? devour soil. circling its bounty desperate brown. in the lost hours you float guilty. eating your own goodbye. now invisible. now from a teaspoon. the connection to survive is always *hold me. let us last it out.*

One Woman-Horse Show

1. Press Night

the moment I finished
the performance was a room
of deja vu, skewed at angles
I was a foal, I was

a wardrobe standing
on ceremony, taking its bow
shrinking into a miniature
or giant version of me

there to count the colours
of a living room
one of them asking:
how?

had I misunderstood
the evening brief?

a line of my partner's friends gawping
as though I'd just left the womb

2. Matinee

you are not thinking
of unending sun
dust streamlined
in afternoon triangles

you are not thinking
of the principal's betrayal
nowhere to go
but open & open

you're working alone
distracted
by a lack of space
above your head

thoughts cannot rise
from proscenium
take more risks
splay your body up a wall

why don't you
attempt something
resembling a rave
clubs for your kind have closed

the director will force a male co-star
to touch you
this was intended as an improvisation
a chance to giddy you up

the actor you understudied
in one of The Tragedies
began spitting
over the title of your book

she hadn't read it herself
but how extraordinarily grotesque
to name white people white
how unjust to reject conversation

3. *Interval*

when a friend disappears
I'm unable to call her back
take aim at our forgiveness

I press rewind. what a button.
interrogate foam around teeth
my wet apology

we have to tend the space between us

animals can't say goodbye
& yes my body knows
it's dying in this scene

I'm sorry I say *I'm sinking*
I feel like a thoroughbred
everyone is watching

knowing all the while

4. The Edinburgh Fringe Festival

there are no miracles here
but a person you love
living long before you met her

one of you will die first
one Easter weekend
between sea & Northern Soul

no miracles as we run
from exclusion, leg it
for our healing

a child suffers when a tea tips over
she's stuck inside
the joylessness of adults

she ached, as I did, for play
the right to chaos & mistake
freedom in a purple vintage car

my mind is bringing out desire
& now we're riding together in Cuba

she's thinking in pumpkin seeds—
are the ones we eat, the ones we plant?

we're tasting blackberries
between our childhoods & a river

returning
to watch the moonlight in our home

suddenly, she was loving me

Notes

Pg 7, 'Jah': *'label me greedy… but seldom seen'* and *'I'm having visions of leaving here in a hearse'* are borrowed from 2Pac's song 'Shed so Many Tears'.

'& whenever you let me hit it, sweet like honey' is from D'Angelo's song 'Brown Sugar'.

Pg 8-9: 'One in Four Cowboys Were Black' takes inspiration from Emma Dabiri's book, *Don't Touch my Hair*.

Pg 13: 'Of hidden frames' takes inspiration from *A Month of Single Frames* by Lynne Sachs, a film made with and for Barbara Hammer.

Pg 15: the title 'Into an impotent guilt' is lifted directly from Momtaza Mehri's 'Collage as a Weapon: Raoul Peck's *Exterminate All the Brutes*' in ArtReview.

Pg 17-18: 'Out of Shot' takes inspiration from Chris Burden's 1971 performance piece 'Shoot'.

Pg 22-24: 'One Woman-Horse Show: 4. The Edinburgh Fringe Festival' borrows lines from Steve Monite's song 'Only You'.

The line 'no miracles here' borrows from The Letter Room's show title: 'No Miracles Here' shown at the Edinburgh Fringe Festival 2017.

'Evolution of a brother gone quiet' won the Ledbury Poetry Prize 2021.

'Falling Short' won Silver in the Creative Futures Writing Prize 2021.

Acknowledgements

Thank you to the editors of the following magazines for publishing earlier versions of some of these poems: *bath magg, Magma, Perverse, Powders Press, Queerlings,* and *Tentacular*. Huge gratitude and thanks to Amy Acre and Jake Wild Hall at Bad Betty.

Thanks to The Poetry School and the teachers whose classes have inspired my development, in particular Wayne Holloway-Smith whose class was instrumental.

A massive thank you to Anthony Anaxagorou for your mentorship and articulations—your artistry never fails to inspire. Thank you to Malika Booker for the kind words about my work.

My heartfelt thanks to Nina Bowers, Maia Elsner, Cecilia Knapp, Gboyega Odubanjo, Julia Webb and April Yee for your generosity and invaluable feedback on some of the poems in this pamphlet. Extra shout out to Arji Manuelpillai for the no messing detail and poetry comradery.

Thank you to Daniel Owusu for the creative allyship and beautiful cover illustration made especially for this pamphlet.

Thank you to the collectives, DIY makers, artists, anarchists, dreamers, visionaries and peers who celebrate my poetry alongside me and who are a joy to share creative space with; namely Southbank Centre's New Poets Collective—you guys are the best and have my deepest admiration. To Brainchild Festival & The Pappy Show for nurturing my poetry experiments and bringing the radical joy.

Thank you Youness Bouzinab, Angelica Burrill, Tom Clark, Zoe Correa, Dino Fetscher, Danielle Henry, Rebecca Forbes Hitchen, Olivia Gagan, Erica Jeffrey, Keziah Joseph, Laurel Marston, Lucy McFadzean, Alexander Nicolaou, Alexandra 'A.J' Owen-Jones, Shiv Rabheru, Ashna Rabheru, Yaël Shavit, Carrie Smithstead, Stella Taylor, Nicola Valvis, Anna Young, Rachel Winters and Yasser Zadeh for your love and support. Thanks especially to Lua Bairstow, my creative soul-mate, for championing me always.

Thank you to Katie Spark. Your unrelenting belief in me, makes the impossible feel possible. Your love, in its action, is transformative.

Thank you lastly, to my dear family.

Milton Keynes UK
Ingram Content Group UK Ltd.
UKHW050109160424
441202UK00004B/71

9 781913 268299